ackground
EMBOSSING
WITH VELLUM

Anja van Laar

UBLISHERS

Contents

Third printing, March 2005
ISBN 90 5877 371 x

This is a publication from
Forte Publishers BV
P.O. Box 1394
3500 BJ Utrecht
The Netherlands

For more information about the
creative books available from
Forte Publishers:
www.forteuitgevers.nl

Publisher: Marianne Perlot
Editor: Gina Kors-Lambers
Photography and digital image editing:
Fotografie Gerhard Witteveen,
Apeldoorn, the Netherlands
Cover and inner design:
BADE creatieve communicatie,
Baarn, the Netherlands
Translation: TextCase, Hilversum,
the Netherlands

Preface

The many positive reactions have led to two new background embossing stencils. In this book, I have used these new stencils, as well as the existing stencils, with vellum and parchment paper. I think this combination produces very pretty cards and it often produces an attractive lace-like effect. By using the existing background embossing stencils in this way, you will discover many new possibilities.

I hope that you will have as much fun with this technique as I did writing this book. Good luck!

Many thanks to Marianne Perlot for her enthusiasm and support, to Woutine, my empathizing typist, for all her work and to all the other members of the support team for their help and patience.

Techniques

Embossing

Place the stencil on the good side of the card. Turn the stencil and the card over and place them on a light box. Copy the illuminated shapes using the embossing stylus. If you wish, use Pergasoft (Pergamano) to make the embossing easier. If you are going to emboss a large area, then lightly rub a candle over the paper

Dark coloured card is also used in this book. Emboss this type of card in the evening, possibly with a brighter light in the light box. If you wish to use a colour which is too dark, emboss lines on the card, because these can be embossed more by touch.

If you wish to emboss a shape on dark paper, then emboss a simple shape. You could, for example, place a copy of the shape on a light coloured piece of paper next to the light box so that you can see how the lines must go. When embossing wavy lines, you must make sure you know where the line will start and end. This can be done by moving the stencil so that it sticks out from under the card or by using a pencil to draw some dots. You will then know approximately where the line will go. Carefully start with a circular movement when embossing vellum to prevent lines and scratches and then increase the pressure until the pattern becomes nice and white. For a larger pattern, start with a large embossing stylus and then go along the edges with a smaller stylus.

3D cutting

First cut the entire picture out. When cutting out the next layer, look to see what you wish to have in the background and do not cut these bits out. Cut out as many layers as you want in the same way. If you use a number of layers, cut the incisions far into the card and cut the front parts out completely. Most of the shapes are stuck on the cards using 3D glue and the pictures are stuck on top. Do not press too hard when using 3D glue to stick the shapes on the card. You can add as much or little glue as you wish under the pictures, depending on the depth that you wish to create. If you put the glue in a syringe, you will have more control over the quantity of glue you apply.

Cutting out shapes and cutting along the lines

The shapes on the cards are made using stencils AE 1205, AE 1206, AE 1209, AE 1210, AE 1211 and AE 1213. First, emboss the shape

1. Materials

2. Embossing vellum

3. Cutting vellum

4. Attaching vellum to a card using a ribbon

on the coloured card that will be on the top and then cut the shape out remaining approximately 2 mm from the embossed line. You can then stick the shape on a card of a different colour and cut the shape out again, leaving a border of a different colour. This allows you to play with colours. When cutting along any embossed line, you must also always remain approximately 2 mm from the line. Do not throw anything away, because almost everything can be reused. Instead of using a knife, you can also cut the shapes and lines out using a pair of scissors.

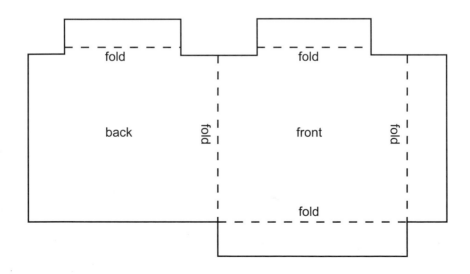

Materials

- ☐ Card: Canson Mi-Teintes (C) and Papicolor (P)
- ☐ Embossing paper
- ☐ Parchment paper
- ☐ Perkacolor
- ☐ Vellum
- ☐ Cutting sheets
- ☐ Background embossing stencils

- ☐ Light box
- ☐ Small embossing stylus
- ☐ Large embossing stylus
- ☐ Cutting mat
- ☐ Knife
- ☐ 3D scissors
- ☐ 3D glue
- ☐ Ruler
- ☐ Hole punch

- ☐ Circle cutter
- ☐ Photo glue
- ☐ Bradletz (mini-split pins)
- ☐ Stickles Gold
- ☐ Organza ribbon
- ☐ Embroidery silk
- ☐ Power Pritt (grey)
- ☐ Gold thread

Nostalgic cards

What you need
- [ ] *Card: pale yellow (P29) and light green (P47)*
- [ ] *Thin Perkacolor: mist (P152)*
- [ ] *Cutting sheets: Rie Cramer (5002 and 5003)*
- [ ] *Embossing stencils: AE 1201, AE 1202,*
   AE 1203, AE 1204, AE 1206 and AE 1207
- [ ] *Hole punch*
- [ ] *Ribbon*
- [ ] *Bradletz*
- [ ] *Decorative stickers*

Card 1

Take a light green double card (13.5 x 13.5 cm). Use stencil 1204 to emboss flowers on Perkacolor (12 x 12 cm). Prick holes in the corners of the Perkacolor and the card using a needle or a prick pen and put Bradletz through them. Stick the picture on a pale yellow circle (Ø 7.5 cm) and use 3D glue to stick it on the card. Use stencil 1206 to emboss the shape on pale yellow card and cut it out leaving a border. Stick the shape on light green card and cut it out leaving a border. Use the hole punch to punch two holes in the card and one hole in the label. Thread a ribbon through the holes and make a pretty bow. Make the picture 3D and stick a decorative sticker on the label.

Card 2

Take a pale yellow double card (13.5 x 13.5 cm) and stick light green card (12.5 x 12.5 cm) on it. Take a piece of Perkacolor (12 x 12 cm) and use stencil 1203 to emboss lilies on it. Stick the picture on a light green circle (Ø 7.5 cm) and use 3D glue to stick it on the Perkacolor. Stick the Perkacolor on the card, making sure the glue is only placed behind the picture. Make the picture 3D.

Card 3

Take a pale yellow double card (13.5 x 13.5 cm). Stick light green card to the rear flap inside the card. Take some Perkacolor (13.5 x 13.5 cm) and use stencil 1201 to emboss dots on it. Use a small amount of Power Pritt to stick this on the light green card. Stick the picture on a piece of light green card and use stencil 1201 to emboss a square around it. Cut the square out leaving a border. Stick the square inside the card in the middle of the front flap. Next, cut around the right-hand half of the square. Fold the front flap of the card double. Use stencil 1207 to emboss stripes on the front flap. Make the picture 3D and stick text stickers on the card.

Card 4

Take a Perkacolor double card (13.5 x 13.5 cm).
Use the lines of stencil 1201 to emboss a square
(7 x 7 cm) in the middle of the card and use
stencil 1202 to emboss the diamonds. Cut the
inside of the embossed square out. Take a light
green double card (13.5 x 13.5 cm) and stick
the picture on it so that it is behind the square
you have cut out. Use the hole punch to punch
two holes in the fold of the card. Thread a
ribbon through the holes and tie it in a bow.
Make the picture 3D.

Pick-me-up cards

What you need
- [ ] *Card: lavender blue (C150) and white (C335)*
- [ ] *Thick and thin Pergamano parchment paper: Fantasy ivory (1652 and 1653)*
- [ ] *Cutting sheets: Picturel 540, 541 and 542*
- [ ] *Embossing stencils: AE 1201, AE 1203, AE 1204, AE 1206, AE 1207, AE 1209, AE 1210, AE 1212 and AE 1213*
- [ ] *Bradletz*
- [ ] *Hole punch*
- [ ] *Organza ribbon*
- [ ] *Embroidery silk*
- [ ] *Decorative stickers*

Card 1

Take a piece of blue card (13.5 x 13.5 cm) and
stick white card (12 x 12 cm) on it. Stick a picture
on the white card. Take thin parchment paper
(11.5 x 11.5 cm) and use stencil 1201 to emboss
dots on it. Place the parchment paper on the card
(where it will finally be stuck on the card) and use
the hole punch to punch two holes. Thread
Organza ribbon through the holes and tie it in a
pretty bow. Stick a decorative sticker on the card.

Card 2

Take a piece of blue card (19.5 x 14 cm) and
fold it 5.5 cm from the top. Use stencil 1207
to emboss the curved line and the stripes.

Cut along the curved line leaving a border. Cut thick parchment paper to the correct size and use Power Pritt to stick it to the front flap of the card. Take a piece of white card (14 x 4 cm) and use stencil 1207 to emboss the curved line. Cut along the line leaving a border and stick it on the card. Use stencil 1207 to emboss some leaves. Stick white card to the rear flap inside the card. Use stencil 1206 to emboss the shapes on white card and cut them out leaving a border. Stick the shapes on blue card and cut them out leaving a border. Use 3D glue to stick them on the card. Make the picture 3D.

Card 3

Take a piece of white card (21.5 x 13.5 cm) and fold it 8 cm from the top. Use stencil 1207 to emboss the line and then cut along the line leaving a border. Cut blue card to the correct size, stick it behind the front flap and cut along the line to leave a border. Cut thick parchment paper to the correct size and use Power Pritt to stick it to the front flap of the card. Take a piece of white card (13.5 x 7 cm) and use stencil 1207 to emboss the line and stencil 1204 to emboss stripes on it. Cut along the line leaving a border. Stick the white card on blue card and cut along the line leaving a border. Stick the card on the

parchment paper. Use stencil 1204 to emboss flowers on the parchment paper. Use stencil 1210 to emboss a cloud on white and blue card and cut them out leaving a border. Stick the white cloud on blue card and cut it out leaving a border. Use 3D glue to stick the clouds on the card. Make the pictures 3D and stick decorative stickers on the card.

Bag 4

Make this bag according to the instructions for the bag in Say it with flowers. Use stencil 1201 and blue card to make the bag. Use stencil 1209, white card and thick parchment paper for the shape.

Card 5

Take a piece of blue card (18 x 13.5 cm) and fold it 3 cm from the left-hand side. Use stencil 1212 to emboss the stripes. Take thick parchment paper (18 x 10.5 cm) and use stencil 1213 to emboss the shape as shown in the photograph. Use stencil 1212 to emboss the wavy line and the flowers. Cut the inside of the shape out and cut along the wavy line leaving a border. Stick the parchment paper to the front flap. Cut a piece of white card to the correct size and stick behind the front flap. Make the picture 3D.

1.

2.

3.

4.

6.

5.

Blue cards

What you need
- ☐ Card: iris blue (P31), lavender blue (C150) and white (C335)
- ☐ Camascio embossing card (pale yellow)
- ☐ Pergamano vellum (1611)
- ☐ Thick Pergamano parchment paper: Fantasy ivory (1653)
- ☐ Cutting sheets - Mattie de Bruine
- ☐ Embossing stencils: AE 1201, AE 1202, AE 1203, AE 1207, AE 1208, AE 1209, AE 1212 and AE 1213
- ☐ Bradletz
- ☐ Organza ribbon
- ☐ Decorative stickers

Card 1

Take an iris blue double card (10 x 10 cm) and use stencil 1212 to emboss stripes on it. Make a vellum double card (13.2 x 13.2 cm) and use stencil 1212 to emboss flowers on it. Use a small amount of Power Pritt to stick the vellum to the inside of the iris blue card. Use stencil 1213 to emboss the shape on Camascio card and cut it out leaving a border. Stick the shape on iris blue card and cut it out leaving a border. Use 3D glue to stick the shape on the card (also apply 3D glue to the vellum). Make the pictures 3D and stick decorative stickers on the card.

Card 2

Take a piece of iris blue card (15 x 10.5 cm). Use stencil 1212 to emboss the wavy line and cut along the line leaving a border. Take a piece of vellum (29.7 x 11 cm). Fold it 10.5 cm from the right-hand side and 8.7 cm from the left-hand side. Use stencil 1212 to emboss the wavy line and the flowers on the right-hand flap. Cut along the wavy line leaving a border, until the fold. Emboss the wavy line on the left-hand flap. The highest point of the wavy line must be 7.5 cm from the bottom of the card. Use stencil 1212 to emboss stripes. Cut along the wavy line, leaving a border, until the fold. Next, cut the middle flap from fold to fold at an angle. Stick the iris blue card to the middle section of the vellum. Cut Camascio card to the correct size, use the Power Pritt to stick it behind the left-hand flap and cut it out leaving a border. Use stencil 1213 to emboss the shape on Camascio card and cut it out leaving a border. Stick the shape on iris blue card and cut it out leaving a border. Use 3D glue to stick the shape on the card as shown in the photograph. Make the pictures 3D and add some decorative stickers.

Card 3 (also on page 3)

Take a piece of Camascio card (19 x 13.5 cm)

and fold it 3 cm from the left-hand side. Use stencil 1207 to emboss stripes on the front flap. Take a piece of vellum (19 x 10.5 cm) and use stencil 1208 to emboss the wavy line on it, moving the stencil to make the line longer. Use stencil 1207 to emboss the leaves as shown in the photograph. Cut along the wavy line, leaving a border, and use the Power Pritt to stick the vellum behind the front flap. Cut iris blue card to the correct size and use a small amount of Power Pritt to stick it behind the front flap. Use stencil 1209 to emboss the shape on vellum and cut it out leaving a border. Stick the shape on iris blue card and cut it out leaving a border. Use a pin to prick a hole in the shape and the card and use a Bradletz to attach the shape to the card. Make the pictures 3D and stick a decorative sticker on the label.

Card 4

Take a piece of iris blue card (18 x 14 cm) and fold it 4 cm from the top. Use stencil 1202 to emboss the wavy line on the front flap, moving the stencil to increase the length of the line. Cut along the line leaving a border. Cut vellum to the correct size and use Power Pritt to stick

it behind the front flap. Take a piece of Camascio card (8 x 3 cm) and use stencil 1202 to emboss the wavy line. Use stencil 1212 to emboss the stripes. Cut along the wavy line leaving a border and stick it on the vellum. Use stencil 1212 to emboss the flowers. Use stencil 1213 to emboss two apples on Camascio card and cut them out leaving a border. Stick the apples on iris blue card and cut them out leaving a border. Use 3D glue to stick them on the card as shown in the photograph. Make the picture 3D.

Card 5

Take an iris blue double card (14 x 14 cm) and stick a piece of Camascio card (13 x 13 cm) on it. Take a piece of vellum (12.5 x 12.5 cm) and fold it as shown in the photograph, remaining 2 cm from the top left-hand and bottom right-hand corners. Use stencil 1203 to emboss lilies as shown in the photograph. Use stencil 1201 to emboss dots. Use Power Pritt to stick the vellum on the card. Use stencil 1213 to emboss two shapes on Camascio card and cut them out leaving a border.
Stick the shapes on iris blue card and cut them out leaving a border. Use 3D glue to stick the

shapes on the card. Make the pictures 3D and stick decorative stickers on the card.

Card 6

Take a piece of parchment paper (18 x 10.5 cm) and use stencil 1203 to emboss lilies as shown in the photograph. Take a piece of lavender blue card (15.5 x 9 cm) and use stencil 1212 to emboss wavy lines. Cut along the lines leaving a border. Take a white card (14 x 9 cm) and use stencil 1212 to emboss wavy lines and stencil 1201 to emboss dots on it. Cut along the lines leaving a border. Place the three layers together. Use a pin to make two holes through them and use Bradletz to secure the layers together. Use stencil 1206 to emboss the shapes on white card and cut them out leaving a border. Stick the shapes on ivory parchment paper and cut them out leaving a border. Use 3D glue to stick the shapes on the card. Make the pictures 3D. Tie the organza ribbon into an attractive bow around the card.

Say it with flowers

What you need
- [ ] *Card: snow white (P30), blossom (P34), Christmas red (P43), thick and thin Brilliant gravel (P161)*
- [ ] *Pergamano vellum: 1715 and 1716*
- [ ] *Cutting sheets: Mattie de Bruine*
- [ ] *Embossing stencils: AE 1212 and AE 1213*
- [ ] *Hole punch*
- [ ] *Organza ribbon (6 mm)*
- [ ] *Embroidery silk*
- [ ] *Decorative stickers*

Card 1

Take a Christmas red piece of card (22 x 10 cm) and fold it 4 cm from the left-hand side. Use stencil 1212 to emboss stripes on the front flap as shown in the photograph. Take a piece of old rose vellum (17.5 x 10 cm) and use stencil 1212 to emboss stripes as shown in the photograph and then emboss the flowers. Stick the vellum behind the front flap of the card. Take a piece of snow white card (18 x 10 cm) and stick it to

the front flap of the card, making sure not to stick it to the vellum. Stick pictures on the snow white card as shown in the photograph. Use stencil 1213 to emboss the shape on gravel card and cut it out. Stick the shape on Christmas red card and cut it out leaving a border. Use a hole punch to punch a hole in it. Tie a piece of Organza ribbon around the card and tie a pretty bow through the shape. Stick a decorative sticker on the label.

Card 2

Take a piece of thick gravel card (24 x 13.5 cm) and fold it 10.5 cm from the top. Use stencil 1212 to emboss wavy lines at an angle. Emboss flowers above the wavy lines. Cut along the wavy lines leaving a border. Cut a piece of Christmas red card to the right size and stick it behind the front flap. Cut the card off in a straight line so that it just protrudes from under the wavy lines. Take a piece of stripy vellum (13.5 x 13.5 cm) and stick it behind the front flap. Stick blossom card

(13.5 x 13.5 cm) behind the front flap, making sure not to stick it to the vellum. Use stencil 1213 to emboss the shape on gravel card. Cut the shape out leaving a border and stick it on Christmas red card. Cut it out again leaving a border and use 3D glue to stick it on the card. Make the picture 3D.

Card 3

Take a thin, gravel double card (10 x 10 cm) and use stencil 1212 to emboss branches around the edges. Cut a square (7 x 7 cm) out of the middle. Cut a piece of Christmas red card to the right size and stick it behind the front flap. Cut the square out to leave a 2 mm wide border. Stick striped vellum behind the opening and stick blossom card behind the vellum to give the vellum a nice colour. Use stencil 1213 to emboss the shape on gravel card and cut it out leaving a border. Stick the shape on Christmas red card and cut it out leaving a border. Use 3D glue to stick the shape on the card and make the picture 3D.

Card 4

Take a piece of snow white card (23 x 14 cm) and fold it 9 cm from the left-hand side. Take a piece of old rose vellum (23 x 14 cm) and also fold it

9 cm from the left-hand side. Use stencil 1212 to emboss the wavy line and then the flowers on the front flap. Cut along the wavy line leaving a border. Place the vellum around the card and use a small amount of Power Pritt to stick it to the back of the card. Cut Christmas red card to the correct size. Use stencil 1212 to emboss stripes on it as shown in the photograph and stick it to the rear flap inside the card.

Use stencil 1213 to emboss the shape on snow white card and cut it out leaving a border. Stick the shape on Christmas red card and cut it out leaving a border. Use a hole punch to punch a hole in the shape.

Tie a piece of Organza ribbon around the front flap of the card and tie a pretty bow through the shape. Make the pictures 3D and stick decorative stickers on the shape.

Card 5

Take a piece of Christmas red card (24 x 10.5 cm) and fold it 4.5 cm from the left-hand side. Stick a piece of thin gravel card (10.5 x 4.8 cm) behind the front flap. Take a piece of old rose vellum (15 x 10.5 cm) and use stencil 1212 to emboss the wavy line and some flowers. Cut along the wavy line leaving a border and stick the vellum behind the front flap. Take a piece of gravel card (19.5 x 10.5 cm) and use stencil 1212 to emboss stripes as far as the wavy line (mark this first with a pencil). Stick the card behind the front flap.

Use stencil 1213 to emboss the shape on snow white card and cut it out leaving a border. Stick the shape on Christmas red card and cut it out leaving a border. Use 3D glue to stick the shape on the card. Make the picture 3D and stick decorative stickers on the card.

Bag 6

Make a bag as shown in the diagram on page 6 (including the folds) from thick gravel card. Use stencil 1212 to emboss flowers on the front of the bag. Take two pieces of embroidery silk (15 cm) and tie a double knot in each piece. Fold the top two strips around the embroidery silk and stick them to the bag. Stick the rear of the bag to the front of the bag using the other two strips. Use stencil 1213 to emboss an apple on Christmas red card and cut it out leaving a border. Take a piece of gravel card (4.7 x 4.3 cm) and stick the apple on it so that more than half of the apple sticks out above the gravel card. Stick a decorative sticker on the apple and slide it into the bag. Use 3D glue to stick a picture on the bag.

Marriage cards

Card 1

Take a piece of lemon card (28 x 10.5 cm) and fold it 8 cm from the left-hand side. Use stencil 1208 to emboss wavy lines and use stencil 1204 to emboss stripes. Cut along the wavy lines leaving a border. Cut a piece of flowery vellum to the correct size and stick it behind the front flap. Cut a piece of lemon card to the correct size and stick behind the front flap. Make the picture 3D.

Card 2

Take a white double card (13.5 x 13.5 cm). Take a piece of Perkacolor (14.5 x 13.5 cm) and fold it 1 cm from the side. Use stencil 1203 to emboss

lilies on the Perkacolor and then stick the 1 cm wide flap to the back of the card. Take a piece of lemon card (19 x 13.5 cm) and fold it 5.5 cm from the right-hand side. Use stencil 1208 to

emboss wavy lines on the small flap 4.5 cm from the fold. Use stencil 1207 to emboss horizontal stripes. Cut along the wavy lines leaving a border and then stick it to the back of the card. Use stencil 1213 to emboss the hat on white card. Cut the hat out leaving a border and stick it on lemon card. Cut it out again leaving a border and use 3D glue to stick it on the card. Make the pictures 3D and stick a decorative sticker on the card.

Card 3

Take a lemon double card (13.5 x 13.5 cm). Make a Perkacolor double card (13.5 x 13.5 cm)

1.

2.

3.

4.

and use stencil 1201 to emboss wavy lines 1.5 cm from the edge. Use stencil 1204 to emboss flowers on the Perkacolor. Cut along the wavy lines leaving a border. Use stencil 1213 to emboss the shape on white card and cut it out leaving a border. Stick the shape on lemon card and cut it out leaving a border. Take a piece of Organza ribbon (2.5 cm), fold it around the two cards and use a piece of double-sided adhesive tape to stick the ends together. Use 3D glue to stick the shape on the card. Only apply the glue where the two ends of the Organza ribbon are stuck together. Make the picture 3D.

Card 4

Take a piece of white card (25.5 x 10.5 cm) and fold it 5.5 cm from the left-hand side.
Use stencil 1203 to emboss wavy lines. Next, use stencil 1201 to emboss horizontal stripes, missing out every third line. Cut along the wavy lines leaving a border. Take a piece of Perkacolor (19.5 x 10.5 cm) and use stencil 1203 to emboss wavy lines on it. Use stencil 1201 to emboss dots as shown in the photograph. Cut along the wavy lines leaving a border. Stick the Perkacolor to the front flap. Cut lemon card to the correct size and stick the picture on it so that it sits behind the Perkacolor. Stick the card to the front flap. Use stencil 1206 to emboss the shape on lemon card and cut it out leaving a border. Make the picture 3D and stick decorative stickers on the label. Use a hole punch to punch a hole in the label and tie Organza ribbon through it.

Tip

Make your own thank you present by putting a sweet in a piece of tulle. Tie Organza ribbon around it and add a label.
Use 3D glue to stick pictures on the label and add a decorative sticker.

Merry Christmas

What you need

- ☐ Card: snow white (P30), night blue (P41) and Christmas red (P43)
- ☐ Thick and thin Perkacolor: mist
- ☐ Cutting sheets: MR 0006 and 0007
- ☐ Embossing stencils: AE 1201, AE 1202, AE 1205, AE 1208, AE 1209 and AE 1213
- ☐ Hole punch
- ☐ Gold thread
- ☐ Bradletz
- ☐ Stickles Gold
- ☐ Decorative stickers

Card 1

Take a piece of Christmas red card (21 x 18 cm) and fold it 3 cm from the left-hand side. Use stencil 1201 to emboss stripes on the small flap. Take a piece of night blue card (21 x 9.5 cm) and stick it to the front flap. Take a piece of thin Perkacolor (21 x 14.5 cm) and use stencil 1201 to emboss wavy lines and dots on it. Cut along the wavy lines leaving a border. Use a small amount of Power Pritt to stick the Perkacolor to the front flap. Use stencil 1205 to emboss the shape on Perkacolor and cut it out leaving a border. Use the hole punch to punch holes in the card and the shape and thread gold thread through

them. Make the pictures 3D and stick decorative stickers on the card.

Card 2

Take a night blue double card (14.8 x 10.5 cm). Take a piece of thin Perkacolor (29.7 x 7 cm) and fold it double. Use stencil 1208 to emboss wavy lines on the front and the back of the Perkacolor and emboss stars on the front. Cut along the wavy lines leaving a border. Use stencil 1213 to emboss the shape on white card and cut it out. Stick the shape on Christmas red card and cut it out leaving a border. Use 3D glue to stick the shape on the Perkacolor. Stick the Perkacolor on the card by only applying glue behind the shape. Make the pictures 3D and add some Stickles Gold to the pictures. Stick decorative stickers on the card.

squares (6 x 6 cm) on thick Perkacolor. Use stencil 1201 to emboss dots on one square and use stencil 1208 to emboss stars on the other square. Cut the squares out (slightly bumpy) leaving a border. Use Power Pritt to stick the squares on the card. Use stencil 1209 to emboss shapes on white and Christmas red card. Cut the shapes out leaving a border. Stick them on card of the other colour and cut them out leaving a border. Use 3D glue to stick the shapes on the card. Make the pictures 3D and add some Stickles Gold to the pictures.

Card 3

Use a night blue double card (13.5 x 13.5 cm). Stick a piece of white card (12 x 12 cm) on the double card and stick Christmas red card (11.5 x 11.5 cm) on the white card. Take a piece of thin Perkacolor (11 x 11 cm) and use stencil 1208 to emboss stars on it. Stick the Perkacolor on the card by only applying glue to the middle of the Perkacolor. Use stencil 1205 to emboss the shape on white card and cut it out leaving a border. Stick the shape on Christmas red card and cut it out leaving a border. Use 3D glue to stick the shape on the Perkacolor. Make the picture 3D and stick decorative stickers on the card.

Card 4

Take a night blue double card (13.5 x 13.5 cm). Use the lines of stencil 1204 to emboss two

Card 5

Fold an A4 sheet of night blue card double. Take a piece of thin Perkacolor (20 x 7.5 cm) and use stencil 1202 to emboss wavy lines on it, moving the stencil to increase the length of the lines. Use stencil 1208 to emboss stars between the wavy lines. Cut along the wavy lines leaving a border. Use Bradletz in the corners to attach the Perkacolor to the double card. Use stencil 1205 to emboss shapes on white card and cut them out leaving a border. Stick two shapes on Christmas red card and cut them out leaving a border. Use 3D glue to stick the shapes on the card. Make the pictures 3D and add some Stickles Gold to the pictures.

It's a boy!

What you need
- ☐ Card: violet (P20), lavender (P21), snow white (P30) and light green (P47)
- ☐ Thin Perkacolor: mist (P152)
- ☐ Eline Pellinkhof vellum: AKV 0015
- ☐ Eline Pellinkhof cutting sheets: baby's 1, baby's 2 and AKL 1005
- ☐ Embossing stencils: AE 1201, AE 1202, AE 1203, AE 1204, AE 1205 and AE 1212
- ☐ Hole punch
- ☐ Organza ribbon (6 mm)
- ☐ Decorative stickers

Card 1

Take a lavender double card (14 x 9 cm). Use stencil 1208 to emboss the wavy lines on it and use stencil 1201 to emboss stripes as shown in the photograph. Cut along the wavy lines leaving a border. Take a snow white double card (10.5 x 9 cm) and fold it around the lavender card. Take a Perkacolor double card (10.5 x 9 cm) and use stencil 1205 to emboss the square on it 1 cm from the bottom and the right-hand side. Use stencil 1202 to emboss diamonds on the Perkacolor. Cut the inside of the square out leaving a border and fold the Perkacolor around the card. Stick the picture behind the cut-out square. Use the hole punch to punch two holes, one under the other. Attach everything together by making a pretty bow with Organza ribbon and stick the dummy to the end of the ribbon. To make the dummy a bit stronger, you can first stick it on card and then cut it out.

Card 2

Take a piece of lavender card (18 x 9 cm) and fold it 3 cm from the left-hand side. Use stencil 1212 to emboss wavy lines on it and use stencil 1204 to emboss stripes. Cut along the wavy lines leaving a border. Cut a piece of light green card to the correct size and stick it behind the front flap. Cut along the wavy lines again leaving a border. Take a piece of Perkacolor (13.5 x 9 cm) and use stencil 1212 to emboss a wavy line and stencil 1201 to emboss dots. Cut along the wavy line leaving a border. Take another piece of Perkacolor (14.5 x 9 cm) and emboss a wavy line on it. Cut along the wavy line leaving a border. Stick the picture on the Perkacolor card. Cut a strip of snow white card to the correct size and use a small amount of Power Pritt to stick the two pieces of Perkacolor to the white card and then to the front flap. Use the hole punch to punch two holes in the card.

Thread Organza ribbon through the holes and tie it in a pretty bow.

Card 3

Take a light green double card (10 x 10 cm) and a piece of lavender card (9 x 9 cm). Use stencil 1201 to emboss stripes on the lavender card and stick it on the light green card. Take a piece of Perkacolor (9 x 8 cm) and fold it 3 cm from the top. Use stencil 1201 to emboss stripes on the big flap. Use stencil 1212 to emboss wavy lines and stencil 1201 to emboss dots on the small flap. Cut along the wavy lines leaving a border. Use the Perkacolor to help you see where to stick the picture. Use Power Pritt to stick the Perkacolor on the card. Tie Organza ribbon into a bow and use 3D glue to stick it on the card.

Card 4

Take a lavender double card (13.5 x 13.5 cm) and use stencil 1202 to emboss wavy lines on it, moving the stencil to increase the length of the bottom line. Use stencil 1201 to emboss stripes between the wavy lines, missing out every third line. Use stencil 1201 to emboss dots. Cut between the stripes and along the wavy lines leaving a border. Cut a piece of snow white card to the correct size and stick it inside the card against the rear flap. Cut vellum to the correct size and use a small amount of Power Pritt to stick it against the fold. Use stencil 1205 to emboss the shape on snow white card and cut it out. Stick the shape on violet card and cut it out leaving a border. Use 3D glue to stick the shape on the card. Use 3D glue to stick the picture on the card. Add some decorative stickers.

Card 5

Take a lavender double card (12 x 12 cm) and use a pencil to draw a large plus sign on the left-hand inside flap of the card, so that it is divided into four. Use stencil 1205 to emboss the squares, using the plus sign as a guide. Use stencil 1203 to emboss lilies in the corners. Cut the inside of the squares out leaving a border. Stick a light green card behind the front of the card. Cut the inside of the squares out again leaving a border. Take a piece of Perkacolor (12 x 12 cm) and stick it behind the front of the card. Cut a piece of snow white card to the correct size and stick it to the right-hand inside flap of the card. Use 3D glue to stick pictures on the card and add some decorative stickers.

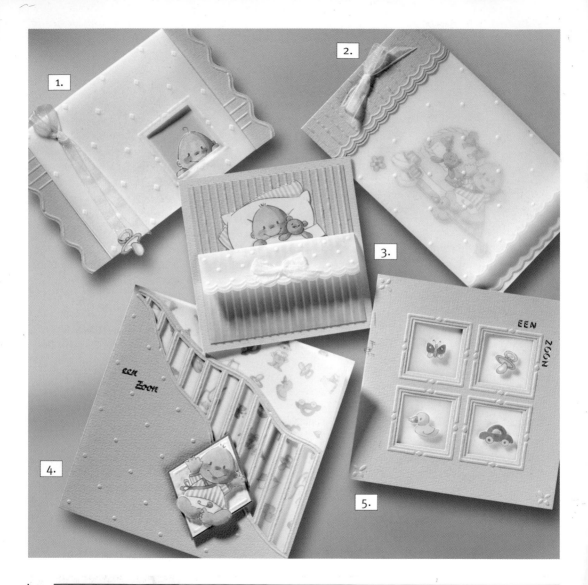

It's a girl!

What you need
- ☐ *Card: carnation white (P03) and cerise (P33)*
- ☐ *Thick and thin Perkacolor: pink*
- ☐ *Marjoleine cutting sheets: bears*
- ☐ *Embossing stencils: AE 1201, AE 1202, AE 1203, AE 1204, AE 1205, AE 1206 and AE 1212*
- ☐ *Hole punch*
- ☐ *Organza ribbon (6 mm)*
- ☐ *Decorative stickers*

Card 1

Take a carnation white double card (13.5 x 13.5 cm) with the fold on the left-hand side. Take a piece of thin, pink Perkacolor (13 x 13 cm) and use stencil 1212 to emboss wavy lines on it as shown in the photograph and use stencil 1203 to emboss lilies. Cut along the wavy lines leaving a border. Take a piece of carnation white card (7 x 7 cm) and stick the picture on it. Stick the card on Perkacolor and stick the Perkacolor on the card, making sure you only apply glue to the Perkacolor behind the picture. Make the picture 3D.

Card 2

Take a piece of carnation white card (29.7 x 9 cm) and fold it 13 cm and 26 cm from the left-hand side. Use stencil 1203 to emboss wavy lines on the small flap and use stencil 1204 to emboss horizontal stripes. Cut along the wavy lines leaving a border. Cut thin, pink Perkacolor to the correct size and use stencil 1204 to emboss flowers on it as shown in the photograph. Use Power Pritt to stick the Perkacolor to the rear of the card. Use stencil 1205 to emboss the shape on cerise card. Cut the shape out leaving a border and use 3D glue to stick it on the card. Stick a picture on the shape.

Card 3

Take a piece of thick, pink Perkacolor (13.5 x 13.5 cm) and use stencil 1204 to emboss flowers on it.
Take a piece of carnation white card (9 x 9 cm) and use the lines of stencil 1201 to emboss a square (8.5 x 8.5 cm) on it. Place this in the middle of the Perkacolor and use the hole punch to punch two holes. Tie a pretty bow through the holes. Make the picture 3D.

Card 4

Take a piece of carnation white card (29.7 x 9 cm) and fold it double. Use stencil 1202 to emboss lines at the top and bottom of the card. Take a piece of thick, pink Perkacolor (29.7 x 7.5 cm) and fold it double with the fold on the left-hand side. Use stencil 1202 to emboss diamonds on it. Place the Perkacolor around the card and use a small amount of Power Pritt (next to the fold) to stick it to the back of the card. Use stencil 1205 to emboss two squares on cerise card. Cut the squares out leaving a border and use 3D glue to stick them on the card. Stick pictures on the squares. Tie the organza ribbon into an attractive bow around the card.

Card 5

Take a thick, pink Perkacolor double card (15 x 10.5 cm) with the fold on the left-hand side and use stencil 1201 to emboss dots on it. Take a carnation white double card (12 x 10.5 cm). Stick the picture on it and slide the carnation white card inside the Perkacolor card. Mark the corners of the picture on the Perkacolor and cut out the square. Use stencil 1206 to emboss a heart on carnation white card and cut it out leaving a border. Stick the heart on cerise card and cut it out leaving a border. Use a hole punch to punch a hole in the label and two holes in the fold of the card. Thread Organza ribbon through the holes and tie it into a pretty bow. Stick decorative stickers on the label.

Fan (page 1)

What you need
- ☐ Card: lavender blue (P21)
- ☐ Thin Perkacolor blue: (P148)
- ☐ Cutting sheets: Forget-me-nots (IT 391)
- ☐ Embossing stencils: AE 1203 and AE 1207
- ☐ Hole punch
- ☐ Wooden spatula
- ☐ Embroidery silk

Take a piece of lavender blue card (13.5 x 11 cm) and use a pencil to mark on the card the two points where the wooden spatula will be. Take stencil 1203 and use these two points to see what the best way to emboss the lines is. Use the pencil to mark a couple of points as a guide, for example, at the start and end of a line.

Once you have done this, you can use these points to start embossing. You can also draw the fan on a piece of paper instead of embossing the lines and then copy the diagram with a pencil. Cut along the lines leaving a border. Cut blue Perkacolor to the correct size.

To do this, you can draw all the way around the fan and then cut the Perkacolor slightly smaller. Use stencil 1207 to emboss some leaves. Apply Power Pritt to the middle of the Perkacolor and also at the bottom where the spatula will go and stick it on the card.

Stick the spatula on the card and make the pictures 3D. Make a cord by twisting together two pieces of embroidery silk. Tie two knots at each end and attach the cord to the wooden spatula.

Many thanks to:
Avec BV in Waalwijk, the Netherlands • Kars en Co BV in Ochten, the Netherlands • Papicolor International BV in Utrecht, the Netherlands • Pergamano International in Uithoorn, the Netherlands for supplying the material.

Shopkeepers can order the materials from the companies listed above.